STAMPS

THEODORE ROWLAND-ENTWISTLE

Topics

The Age of the Dinosaurs
Bridges
Castles
Earthquakes and Volcanoes
Energy
Farm Animals
Great Disasters
Houses and Homes
Jungles
Maps and Globes
Money

Peoples of the World
Pollution and Conservation
Religions
Robots
Shops
Spacecraft
Stamps
Television
Trees of the World
Under the Ground

All the words that appear
in **bold** are explained in the
glossary on page 30.

First published in 1986 by
Wayland (Publishers) Ltd
61 Western Road, Hove
East Sussex BN3 1JD

© Copyright 1986 Wayland (Publishers) Ltd

Phototypeset by
Kalligraphics Ltd, Redhill, Surrey
Printed in Belgium by
Casterman sa, Tournai

British Library Cataloguing in Publication Data
Rowland-Entwistle, Theodore
    Stamps. – (Topics)
    1. Postage-stamps – History – Juvenile literature
    I. Title   II. Series
    769.569   HE6182

ISBN 0–85078–822–6

Contents

The Purpose of Stamps

This Canadian stamp was printed during the reign of Queen Victoria.

A stamp was originally an official mark stamped or pressed on to a document, in much the same way as

a rubber stamp is used today. When you travel abroad an **immigration officer** stamps your passport in this way. Some stamps impress a design into the paper, rather than make a mark on the surface. These are often used on legal papers, such as the documents used for buying and selling houses. The stamp usually

British Soldiers guarding a delivery of stamped legal papers against crowds of angry colonists who resented the stamp tax imposed on them.

shows that a tax – sometimes called stamp duty – or a fee has been paid.

Stamp duty led to war on one famous occasion. In 1765 the British Parliament passed an **Act**, the Stamp Act, to impose taxes on Britain's thirteen North American colonies. Britain needed the money that such a tax would raise to pay for an army to guard the colonies. The people who lived in these settlements were made to pay stamp duty on such items as newspapers, college diplomas, calendars, playing cards and

Various types of stamps can be bought from Philatelic Centres, which are found in most post offices.

dominoes. This was one of several Parliamentary Acts which led the colonies to rebel against Britain and declare the independence of the United States.

The kind of stamp we all know is the postage stamp. It shows that a fee has been paid to the Post Office for the delivery of a letter or parcel. Most postage stamps are **adhesive**, that is they have gum on the back and can be stuck on any package. Many businesses use **franking** meters, machines hired from the Post Office. These record the amount to be paid directly on to each envelope.

Adhesive stamps are used for purposes other than postage. Post Offices issue savings stamps, so that people can put money aside in a bank or to pay for telephone bills and television licences. Some shops issue trading stamps which customers can collect and exchange for goods or money.

Early Postal Systems

Our word 'post' comes from the Latin word *posita* which means something placed. In Roman times messengers and horses were placed at intervals, or posts, along a highway. A letter or parcel would be carried from one post to another until reaching its destination. When coaches were first used to carry letters, the vehicles were drawn by relays of horses known as post-horses. Mail, another name for post, comes from an old French word *male*, meaning a bag, and

Many years ago letters were carried in coaches, pulled by relays of horses.

originally referred to the bag in which letters were carried.

The first postal systems were set up by the rulers of ancient peoples. They were used to carry messages to and from the governors of outlying provinces. Posts of this kind existed in Egypt more than 3,000 years ago and flourished in China, India and Persia (modern Iran) more than 2,000 years ago. In Europe the Romans had an efficient system of posts and couriers (messengers) to carry

The Romans used couriers to carry their letters.

letters across their vast empire.
Urgent letters were carried by men
on horseback.

After the Roman Empire
collapsed in AD 476, it became more
difficult to send letters across
Europe. Roads were bad, and
robbers were likely to waylay
messengers. During the Middle
Ages, merchants used to send
several copies of their letters by
different routes, in the hope that
one would get through.

Nineteenth century highwaymen would stop people on the road and steal their letters or parcels.

A nineteenth century postman was paid by the people to whom he delivered letters.

In the fifteenth century, countries such as France and England began to set up their own postal systems. These were known as State Posts. The Russian State Post started even earlier. The United States organized an efficient postal service almost as soon as it gained its independence in 1776.

A few private systems for the transport of letters were set up. In 1680 a merchant called William Dockwra organized a penny postal service for London. After a few years, however, his business was taken over by the Duke of York (later King James II), who claimed to be the only person who could have a postal service.

By the beginning of the nineteenth century, people in Britain paid the postman for letters they received, not for those they sent. The further a letter travelled the more they had to pay. Members of the House of Lords could send their mail free by franking (signing) the outside of the letters.

Poor people used various methods to escape paying a lot of money for letters. They would put secret marks on the outside of a letter. The person receiving it would glance at the **cover**, see by the signs that all was well, and then refuse to accept or pay for the letter.

In the nineteenth century, letter writing was common among the upper and middle classes, but most poor people could not read and write.

The First Postage Stamps

In 1837 a former schoolmaster named Rowland Hill suggested that the British Government could make more money from the post by charging less for delivery, because this would encourage more people

Rowland Hill, whose ideas inspired the first postage stamps.

to send letters. He also proposed that the price of the postage should be the same whatever the distance, and should vary only according to the weight of the package. Finally, he said all letters should be paid for by the senders, which would save time and trouble for the postmen, who would not have to collect the fees.

Hill's ideas were carried out in 1840. First of all, the postal rate was set at 1d (less than ½p). Then on 6 May 1840 the Post Office

In a nineteenth century post office letters were sorted by hand. Nowadays machines are used.

issued covers (wrappers) in which letters could be enclosed. These covers could be bought from post offices, and are known as Mulready Covers after the artist who designed them. The Post Office also issued adhesive labels which could be stuck on any envelope to pay for the postage. These were the first postage stamps.

Stamps and covers were issued in two values: 1d black and 2d blue.

The first envelopes looked like this, and were designed by William Mulready.

W. MULREADY, R.A.

JOHN THOMPSON.

The first postage stamp to be used was the 'Penny Black'.

The 1d black became known as the 'Penny Black'. Hill thought that most people would use the covers, but, in practice, stamps were preferred. The colour of the 1d stamp was changed from black to red in 1841. This was because black postmarks, marks which the Post Office presses on the letter to show the date, did not show up on it.

At first the new stamps were only for use in Britain, so there was no

Nowadays, almost every country in the world produces stamps.

need to have the name of the country on them. This tradition has been followed ever since. The second country to issue postage stamps was Brazil, in 1843. Its first issues also had no name on them, and neither did the first stamps of Switzerland, produced in 1850. The Swiss post office could not decide which of the country's three languages – German, French and Italian – to use, in case it offended the speakers of the other two. Eventually it decided to use the old Latin name for the country, Helvetia, which is still used today.

Other countries to issue stamps include the United States (1847, but there was a local issue in New York in 1842), Bermuda (1848) and France and Belgium (1849).

Stamps from (left to right) Bermuda, France and the United States.

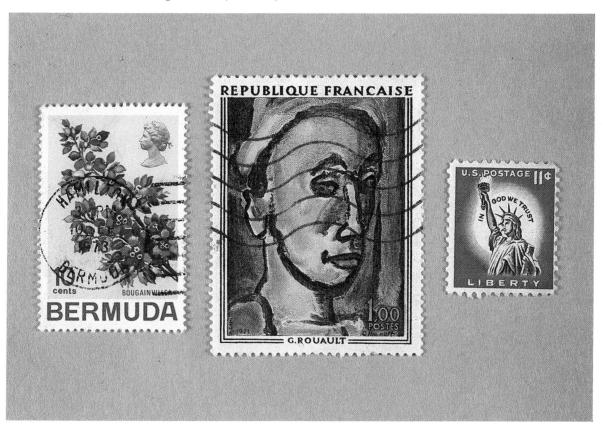

Stamp Collecting

Philatelists are people who collect and study stamps. People have been collecting stamps almost from the time they were first issued. In 1841 a young lady advertised for used stamps to wallpaper her dressing-room! By 1861 a Frenchman, Oscar Berger-Levrault, published the first **catalogue**. It listed nearly 1,500 different stamps from various countries. Today's catalogues list more than 220,000 stamps.

Left *This lady found a rather unique way of using stamps as wallpaper.*

Right *Philatelists are people who collect and study stamps.*

Stanley Gibbons, one of the most famous early stamp collectors.

One of the most famous early collectors was Stanley Gibbons, who began his hobby in 1855, at the age of fifteen. A year later he began dealing in stamps. Soon after, he bought a sack from two sailors, containing two million triangular stamps from the Cape of Good Hope colony. He sold most of them for less than one penny each.

Early collectors tried to obtain an example of every stamp. Nowadays, because there are so many different kinds of stamps, collectors sometimes choose one particular type. Some collect stamps which follow a certain theme, such as pictures of birds or trains. These are known as **thematic collections**. It is great fun to collect examples of the stamps of as many different countries as you can. In this way you can learn a lot of

Some people collect stamps only from certain countries.

Franklin D. Roosevelt

Franklin D. Roosevelt, a former president of the United States was a keen stamp collector.

geography and history.

Collectors put their stamps in **albums**, using hinges made of transparent paper which do not damage the stamps. If a stamp collection is arranged carefully it can look very attractive.

Stamps are found in either mint or used condition. **Mint stamps** are in the same condition as you buy them at the Post Office, with the full **gum** on the back. **Used stamps** bear a **postmark** and have no gum. An unused stamp is one that carries no postmark, but may have lost some of its gum.

Among the many famous people who have collected stamps are Franklin D. Roosevelt, who was President of the United States from 1933 to 1945, and King George V of Britain. King George's collection has been continued by his granddaughter, Queen Elizabeth II.

Printing and Using Stamps

Post Offices have to take great care over the way their stamps are printed. Security is strict at printing works to prevent stamps being stolen. The printers have to check production at every stage to avoid misprints. Sometimes errors do get into circulation, and they are eagerly sought by some collectors. One famous error was made with the British 2½d stamp, issued to commemorate the Silver Jubilee of King George V in 1935. Some of

Stamps were issued to celebrate the Silver Jubilee of King George V, in 1935.

the stamps were printed in the wrong shade of blue. These now fetch more than one hundred times as much as those printed in the correct shade.

There are various methods of printing stamps, but they all involve making a design on a metal plate, known as a printing plate. This plate is coated with ink, and paper is pressed on to it.

Stamps were originally produced on printing presses like this.

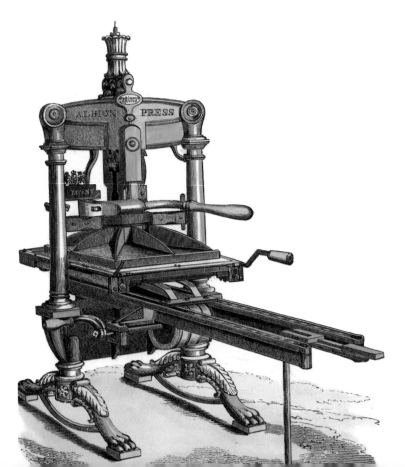

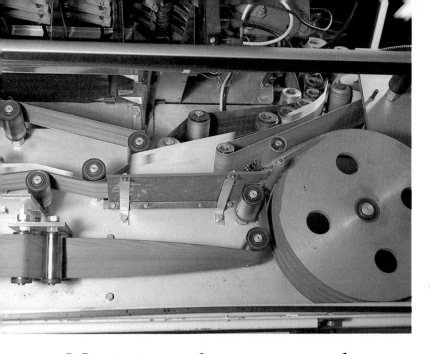

Stamps are put into automatic sorting machines, which can detect if any have been forged.

Most stamps have gum on the back, so that when licked they can be stuck on an envelope. A few countries have issued stamps which have a backing sheet. When you peel it off a sticky surface is revealed. To prevent forgery many stamps are printed on paper with a **watermark** – a design on the paper which only shows up when the stamp is held up to the light. British stamps have 'invisible' bands of a substance called **phosphor** printed across them. This glows under ultraviolet light and can be detected by automatic sorting machines.

The Pony Express service carried mail on horseback across the United States, from Missouri to California.

It is not only individual countries that issue stamps. The **United Nations** produces stamps for its own use in the post office at its headquarters in New York. For some years Kenya, Uganda and Tanzania issued some of their stamps jointly. Unofficial organizations also issue stamps. One famous example was the Pony Express service, which carried mail across the United States from Missouri to California, in 1860 and 1861. The letters bore a 10 cent U.S. government stamp, plus a $5 Pony Express stamp.

More than 150 countries belong to the Universal Postal Union. This was formed in 1878 to improve the international postal system. It is governed by the United Nations, which controls the flow of letters and parcels between different countries and sets the rates that should be charged.

The United Nations building in New York.

Glossary

Act of Parliament A law made by Parliament and approved by the Queen.

Adhesive An adhesive stamp has a substance on the back which becomes sticky when licked.

Album A book in which to put stamps.

Catalogue A list of all the stamps and their prices.

Cover An envelope or other wrapper for a letter.

Franking A mark, put on a letter by a machine, which shows that the postage has been paid.

Gum The sticky substance on the back of a stamp.

Immigration officer The official who checks on people coming into a country which is not their own.

Mint stamp One that is in perfect condition and has not been used.

Phosphor A substance which glows under a special light.

Postmark A mark which cancels a stamp and shows when and where a letter was posted.

Thematic Collections A collection of stamps illustrated with one theme, such as pictures of birds or trains.

United Nations International organization of independent states, formed in 1945 to promote peace and co-operation between member countries.

Used stamp One which has been used for post and has a postmark.

Watermark A design which is impressed on to paper. In the case of stamps, it is used as a precaution against forgery.

Books to Read

All-Colour Book of Stamps by Kenneth Chapman and Barbara Baker (Octopus, 1974)

A More Expeditious Conveyance: The Story of the Royal Mail Coaches by Bevan Rider (J.A. Allen, 1984)

Collecting Postal History by Prince Dimitry Kandaouroff, translated and edited by William Finlay (Peter Lowe, 1973)

Collecting Stamps by Alan James (Basil Blackwell, 1973)

How About Stamp Collecting by John Craven and Richard West (E.P. Publishing, 1979)

Introducing Postal History by A.J. Branston (Stanley Gibbons, 1978)

Philatelic Terms illustrated by Russell Bennett and James Watson (Stanley Gibbons, 1978)

Stamp Collecting by Ian F. Finlay (Ladybird, 1969)

The Post by Alan James (Batsford, 1970)

Picture Acknowledgements

Bruce Coleman 29; Mary Evans 9, 11, 12, 13, 15; Stanley Gibbons 22; Julian Moss 18, 19; Post Office 8, 10, 14, 16, 17, 25, 27; John Tophan 4; R.J. Turner 6–7, 24; Malcolm Walker 20, 21; Wayland Picture Library 5, 26; Peter Newark's Western Americana 28.

Index